I0151995

A DIARY OF ALTERED LIGHT

A DIARY OF
ALTERED LIGHT

POEMS

James Applewhite

Louisiana State University Press
Baton Rouge

For my grandchildren
Christian, Will, Cameron, and Livia

This publication is supported in part
by an award from the
NATIONAL
ENDOWMENT National Endowment for the Arts.
FOR THE ARTS

Published by Louisiana State University Press
Copyright © 2006 by James Applewhite
All rights reserved
Manufactured in the United States of America
First Printing

Designer: Laura Roubique Gleason
Typeface: Adobe Caslon with Trajon Display
Printer and binder: Edwards Brothers, Inc.

Library of Congress Cataloging-in-Publication Data
Applewhite, James.
   A diary of altered light : poems / James Applewhite.
      p. cm.
   ISBN 0-8071-3126-1 (alk. paper) — ISBN 0-8071-3127-x (pbk. : alk. paper)
   I. Title.
PS3551.P67D53 2006
811'.54—dc22

2005016505

The author gratefully acknowledges the editors of the following publications,
in which some of these poems first appeared: *Carolina Quarterly:* "After
Hurricane Floyd," "Last Night We Saw *South Pacific*"; *Chattahoochee Review:*
"Entropy Border," "Joan Crawford and Others"; *North Carolina Literary Review:*
"Ceremony at Heroes' Square," "Christmas by the River," "Fall Will," "Looking
Up from the Woodland Clearing," "River-Ruin," "The Vanished Farmhouse";
Oxford American: "Azaleas by Birdbath," "Documentary"; *Sewanee Review:* "The
Book of Evening," "The Girl in the Mind"; *South Atlantic Quarterly:* "Against
an Ocean Horizon," "Aging/Healing," "Geese by a Drying Lake," "Science
Fiction Sequence"; *Southern Review:* "Birdfoot," "Hank Williams Dream,"
"Rain From a Hurricane."

The paper in this book meets the guidelines for permanence and durability of
the Committee on Production Guidelines for Book Longevity of the Council
on Library Resources. ∞

CONTENTS

A DIARY OF ALTERED LIGHT

Joan Crawford and Others

An actress surviving black and white nitrate
      persists as hairline and cheeks in stills—
more real, perfected, than when passionate
      breath animated her nostrils.

So memory understands backwardly—
      arrests a flicker of moving frames.
A lover's irises widen to see
      a child join shapes and names.

Earlier, your eyes burned intensely
      blue in porch dark over the velvet coat
when I struck a match for the candle. Sky
      of all summer above the boat

aureoled you, the woman I would marry—
      already implicitly flanked by sons
and a daughter. So love retrospectively
      establishes the triptych of icons.

But days as they change and change us
      move over in sun and rain, eroding
clean profile, firm chin—the seasonal process
      a film before editing.

A snapshot of you in a wedding dress
      in dust on the piano doesn't alter.
Like a figure seen from a train, this stillness
      moves our lives along faster.

We scheme for an evening's love-conclusion
      like a last-inning hit or brilliant basket,
but carelessly written scenes drag on
      without the defining moment.

Pyramids, Crusades, the Roman Empire's
      sieges, holy wars and victory fires
abash us in their Technicolored portrayal.
      Lancelot never finds the grail

but gets a girl. Ingrid's eyelids, rising,
        outweigh elephants, airplane-wings—
though the fascist director demands
            legions of extras, foreign lands.

Belated

The erotic puppet dances my gut,
           enraged that he's strung to an image
too late. Desire he can only represent
              descends from another age.

Words decide, when love's realized in time.
           Elegy haunts the approach. White breasts
shock me in the moonlit room when one
              not quite the first one wrests

me back to stand (then lie) in this moment,
           even as I am, grandfather, husband,
lover again, the longed-for absent
              in what is, as bodies understand.

Later, through the window, a bluebird's arc
           in air above the birdbath originates
flying in thought: this meaning-mark
              what memory perpetuates.

The Slant of Light

Alive in these humdrum latter-day days
       I read with my sandwich at *Subway*.
I come outside to a sky's amazing blaze—
         a color I must not say

anymore—*azure* now quaintly unreal.
       Still I love and yearn, make rhyme
of time. Brightly inexorable,
         it replaces disavowed dream.

My mind supplies the invisible:
       those degrees the planet's axis leans
from perpendicular to the orbital
         plane, as it spins

in the heaven of sun-illumination.
       Rotating the days of a year around
its star, this dynamo of time-generation
         electrifies the local ground

I stand on. Leaves feel descent in prospect
       though growth seems all this moment—
the dogwoods richly sufficient.
         Autumn's a distant thought.

But in August, I'll see the oaks turn dull
       before glowing October-purple;
I'll remember this May, that's almost summer,
         and foresee November,

when dogwoods shine ineffable
       time under its altering angle—
as sun moves leaves toward falling
         and *golden* holds a green mourning.

A Sad Heart at the Supermarket

Though a moment begins time once again,
    today's handwriting looks the same,
reinscribing places I've already been—
        checks I've signed with my name

following along aisles, to predictable shelves.
    Asparagus, celery, Darjeeling, Keemun,
distinguish a self from selves
        I resemble—aging, human,

inflected by genes and a cultural dreaming.
    Astounded by my identity among equivalent
others, I think, "April in Paris," humming—
        distinctive as a fingerprint,

I hope—but hardly unique. What is it—
    our fate—to be common in uncommonness—
conscious, in an almost-infinite
        time-expanding universe?

Je est un autre said Rimbaud.
    Wood wakes up as the violin each is.
I remember the moments, when I'd know
        these grainy identities

as roles we have come to, half-aware.
    I saw three kids in a field from the air:
experiencing everything that birth had meant,
        understanding us and the grass in descent.

Birdfoot

A birdfoot violet has seeded itself
        beneath our spreading hydrangea.
So life goes on self-interestedly,
            as capital seeks opportunity.

A reservoir filled by spring rains
        holds water for our house. Movie screens
magnify mounded breasts under gristly
            nipple, for voyeurs seeking bodily

beauty. I hoard what seasons have left,
        cool in the shadowy parlor while
outside sun browns the lawn toward August.
            Stories for grandkids kill

the precious afternoon, preserved when past
        in the silence after, black and white
nitrate wound in the mind's vault—
            reel for the projectionist

of memory—images mortal as the times
        recorded, though script-geometries
stand formal as the pyramids. A balsa plane
            with rubber band spreads its wires

on the dining table. Outside, a cardinal
        pivots his triangle crest on birdbath-
rim as if I'd wound him—as if
            the enactment of a principle.

The business of sun begins
        on crape myrtle bloom, a day lily burns
orange and red-brown. Bees move in little
            white rooms of petal

as sun denies and confirms its going-
        down in rising. *All* will be as it was,
one more time. I won't see not being.
            Will the light seem to pause?

The world, without me to see it,
      is what I can't imagine—quiet,
as if after my grandson's tumult.
         He makes me happy this moment.

How We Fall

Gorgeously they dive into oblivion.
      They rise above the common condition
and plummet, the radar screen holding
          wife, sister-in-law, then nothing.

Memory frames a President's son
      saluting his father with three-year-old hand.
The droning drums and horse-drawn caisson
          align us as mourners. We stand

shoulder to shoulder, in crowds, as when Lincoln's
      train-borne coffin passed. The nation's
leader is broken, our oneness in loss known
          only as he passes on.

Now I doubt whether this blank event
      is a thing I've felt. In confusion,
I fear that the harsh public light
          changes fact into fiction.

Yet the brightness that haloes a dying magnifies
      one day, camera lights glaring in our eyes—
might not making right (we all taken for no reason)
          nor smallness consolation.

The Book of Evening

for Jan

Light lay on the page of the bed turned
        to evening. Silvered by a black-green,
panes cast us onto the yard. Night hovered
           where a poplar towered, then began

descending in a slow draining—lawn,
        azaleas and trees leaking minute by minute
into space. A swallow crossed the skylight;
           beech leaves lost their outline.

Air looked on my words from afar,
        compassionate, graying with the Earth's turning.
Our room let in the outside with glass a star
           could pierce. Slowly my reading

was taken from the book as I sat. Our sheet
        turned down marked one more day. A white
lay without print, for our bodies to write
           their dreaming on all night.

Still an immanence thought our ending not
        complete, this dimming that might be morning
from its color on the lawn but was *becoming*
           as we felt it, a hinge, of changing light.

Last Night We Saw *South Pacific*

I wake to see a cardinal in our white
       crape myrtle. My eye aches. Bees celebrate
morning come with their dynamo-hum
              around a froth of bloom.

Though presently it's paradise for the bees,
       noon will reach ninety-nine degrees.
Le vierge, le vivace et le bel aujourd' hui
              will stultify hope in ennui.

I watched *Raging Planet* on TV.
       Earth's orbit around the sun appears
to alter every hundred thousand years.
              Each thirty million years,

mass extinctions attend Earth's
       traverse of the galactic plane.
The asteroid rain that cratered the moon
              returns, brings species' deaths.

In the Hudson Bay region of Quebec,
       the Laurentide ice sheet
only a geological eye-blink
              ago lay two miles thick.

Disasters preceded us, like violent parents.
       Pangaea's fragmenting land mass
drowned origins like lost Atlantis:
              an enigma for consciousness.

These continents will re-collide
       in their rock-bending tectonic dance,
as once before Tyrannosaurus died.
              So change continues by chance,

as if meaningless—granite to sand,
       sand to sandstone, sandstone to sand.
In five billion years, the sun will expand,
              to Venus and Mars, then end

planet Earth. The hydrangea blooms
        its dry blue, burns a brown lavender.
Earth whirls in space and August comes—
        this slanted light my calendar.

As I water the pink phlox, I wonder
        what use there is for a world of matter—
why the universe exploding into being invents
        night and star-incandesence?

We are the part of it that feels it,
        thinks it, seeing this time in its slant
on bloom with our physical brains that
        change it as they sense it.

We *become*. We hum a story as tune,
        in sonata form that runes this sphinx-
riddle sequence as notes that the pharynx
        fluctuates, to *mean*.

So "This Nearly Was Mine" assuages,
        braced against old loss and war.
Emile de Becque sounds rich with knowledge
        of children and love, before.

Hank Williams Dream

> The exile returns home
> —*The Sleepers*

We tumble in bus station cardboard, suitcase
       or package or a child's game in leaves—
wind's memory beyond this everywhere-place
       of doors like holes in sieves.

So we dream inside them, the bottomless
       looks of glass, closets with knobs where if
thinking enters, a diaphanous octopus
       eyes and grasps with wisps.

Wives' knives shine in bathroom-porcelain
       hard as an SS Commandant, priceless
whiteness. The reflector with bulb waits plain
       at a corner, beside oven and gas.

Beyond, barbed wire and machine gun. Higher
       in the cloud we wheel with crows, loud
in protest, *hated* we say *hated*, choir
       enraged at pain that God allowed.

In the rooms we're someone else, time
       after time. Lean bodies grow cartoon bellies,
Dagwood yells at Blondie, scenes then rhyme
       with bombs, gentlemen and ladies

in hectic sleep. Roiled with dark
       we collide in Packard convertibles that Clark
Gable leaned on, jumping from windows see
       wives wave goodbye like laundry

on clotheslines, Depression, dust bowl, the pelvic
       examination with skeleton articulate
and laughs on us who thought the one slick
       skin job we lived in sufficient.

It streams, an undertone, a half-life in common
        people accept asleep and wake to forget but suspect
from the look on a neighbor's face, guiltily human.
           We roll in our boxes, derelict,

whiskery, Hank Williams' starved song crying
        the unheard-of Europes, the going home
to England, Ireland, Russia, Poland, surviving
           winning loving dying. The long time.

Documentary

I picture the town photographically,
      carry its years in my head: glare-flood,
transparent gold that burned the wood
         of houses and churches fiercely.

A pane of noon sun fell full
      beyond the eaves like a substance, a crystal
metal encrusting leaves. Imponderable
         beginning made visible.

Together on the porch, our torso-shadows
      flattened on the planks like paint.
Deeper in, grandfather's silhouette
         printed the windows.

We suffered a Sunday light, so ideal
      we could not act within it, only exist
as a tribute to its history, only feel
         a judgment-glare persist

through seasons of mules and tobacco leaves,
      Thanksgiving parlors, black men harvesting
in chiaroscuro—perspective that deceives,
         unfathomed by remembering.

It is afternoon always, always the sun
      illuminates changeless ways. We've begun
the same day again, we strain to stay
         as once we were, as we and they,

a photo in white and black, a pageant
      enacted through us, innate, inherited,
sun by sun, each moment. So caught,
         we're cave shadows projected

from paradigms behind: progenitors
      whose blazing substance empties the form
bequeathed. Farmers without futures, war-losers.
         Proprietors of time.

Grandson's Birthday

Math is belief. Ideas dance with experience.
        By the inverse square of their distance,
gravitationally attracted masses enact
              both Newton's constructs, and strict

consequences of beginning constants.
        The planets observed by Kepler
described orbits there to discover—
              not as stone commandments

but as force and mass correspondence
        reflecting initiating limits,
without which the universe would vanish—
              our life not having had chance

to appear. The Anthropic Cosmological
        Principle defines life's seeing as central.
Not knowing all stars like an angel,
              we're cognitive, mortal,

feeling the light in its seasonal slant.
        We observe, kill, mistake ourselves, taste
and take, whirl in love and taint
              our lives with lust and haste.

We suffer with the changing season,
        as August dries the dogwoods' green,
to fall without color this year, though soon
              it may rain, or trees lean

brownly toward winter. Through the window,
        crape myrtles recover whiteness after
wrens ate the Japanese beetles. Shadow
              of a hickory falls sooner

each afternoon. We round toward autumn,
        our family separately voyaging
in similar vessels on a common ocean.
              We celebrate occasions, sing

the happy birthday song that frightens Will,
        who thinks us his communion of saints—
collective, powerful, an archetype that haunts
            him among shadows on the cave wall.

Rain from a Hurricane

In wandering remnants, a hurricane
        brought us whole Septembers of rain.
Our stream now rushes, echoing
           downpour, staying and going.

Yet our heads are where time races
        or jumps or is almost stasis.
Thought makes drama of form, catches
          a red leaf as sign of the universe's

drift, adds *what if* to seasons past,
        imagining when nothing will be left
of the Earth or a life—this agon of budding
          and shedding beginning in ending.

So the season completes itself. Our grandson
        and I walked yesterday on the ridge
past a stream. He seemed his father, a son
          again as we threaded that edge

against horizon, and I mistook the day for one
        thirty years earlier. Then Christian
turned his face as himself, the expression
          of eyes, brow, mouth, his alone.

Now dogwoods and maples prepare, they thin
        September's look in altered air and vein
away chloroplasts. Summer attenuates,
          hinting of underlying scarlets.

I welcome the other autumns I foresee—
        but only those nearest, not yet the last.
Now it's cool enough on the porch for coffee.
          Sun brings seasons past,

yet with a tint, a different quality—
        so faint, that my eye may be inventing.
This slant to slow a wandering bee
          strings space on its tensioning.

After Hurricane Floyd

The TV reported biblical floods
      drowning cities, villages and piney woods.
Now through our propeller's sheen,
        tin roofs gleam an estuarine

horizon. Fields and forests drift,
      entangled in the currents flowing east.
A river surrounds a cemetery and steeple,
        islanding pigs with their people

at the cut-off farmhouse. Refuse
      mats against cars with logs, as the Neuse
overpasses limits, deluge-delirious.
        Barns separate in a victorious

brown sheet that the clouds plate. Our shape
      shadows a submerged road where cars creep,
trailing wakes like boats. Windows and porches
        look on lawns, that sun scorches

through three feet of live creek.
      Second stories drift off to sleep as sleek
ripples coil them. Tractors in sloughs
        plow quickly vanishing rows.

Near metal sheds, a hog farm's effluent
      fans a Pepto-Bismol pink into the current,
unfurling its nasty plume downstream.
        Pigs rosy as in a dream

ride a metal roof, sunburned bathers.
      I imagine grandfathers and great grandfathers,
unable to swim from capsized skiffs those years ago,
        below the marble rows

that hold out still on a fenced knoll
      beside one brick church, as torrents roll
historically seaward. Two tobacco rows
        cast their parallel glows

as if yellow-green soldiers standing at attention.
        An attack and retreat exceeds dimension.
But the land is not swept clean, men
             who farmed hogs will again

brim lagoons with liquid waste, the past
        will insist on houses and lives cast
in the old molds: blacks in downhill shacks
             near creeks and railroad tracks,

their faces held skyward while hope flashes
        as quickly over as our plane's image passes
where a bridge is submerged, then vanishes
             coastward. All I imagine

is in vain, though I suffer this inarticulate
        East again in language. Its sites originate
new recognition and failure as I see land
             emerge and a river wind

like the serpent returned, through New Bern,
        in this long-ruined place where I learn
by error if at all. Boat-furrow tills
             an alluvial drift of ills.

A highway-bridge arises like thought
        over the muddy mix and our flight
turns back from apocalypse. Hurricane Floyd
             seems history, flood to avoid

or endure, stained by hog manure. We'll raise
        more tombstones above it in continuing days
as this seaward streaming reflects us
             winged—runs brown and mysterious.

Entropy Border

A pine shines its needles keen on
      a high blue. A grasshopper marks the season,
spreading antennae toward our door,
        extending only splendor

toward an autumn almost begun—the writing
      spider in our garden waiting
with its zipper stitch of whiter
        thread to spell out winter.

Then a nuthatch bobs on a twig,
      replays his landing on this spring,
and glints into flight again, leaving.
        Overhead, the sky looks big

with time's surprise: this continuous
      change unfolding in fractal bits.
Hoarding sun with photosynthesis,
        an orange leaf hints

at October. In ignorance and trust
      I spin within light of a slight weight
whereby the matter-energy thrust
        turns a circumference from its point.

A single cicada whirrs belatedly of
      winding down in seasons, of love
that longs-for as its mode of being,
        declining in an immense beginning.

A Steeple at Sunset

The cross on a spire against the sky
      marks seasonal blue as with a key.
There history and space intersect,
        locating the absolute act

of a man who was God, and yet died.
      This church scribes the sky with white wood:
coordinates for the ascent of this Son.
        The steeple seems a beacon,

lighted from inside. As his father's Word,
      he descended into time in this land,
then left his lighthouses to stand,
        illuminating the journey's end.

Intrepid traveler, the soul
      sees a narrowing tower as its goal—
perspective on distance, sharpening to a cross
        against the sunset-gloss.

There birdwings flash, past
      shadowing pines. Maples turn red in October,
crows caw at clouds, that cover and uncover,
        while spirit gasps *at last, at last.*

Autumn Banner

Acorns fall with a solid *plop*
       as I walk by. A maple tips
its branches with muted maroon. The tulip
          poplar, still green, keeps

its golden, inner leaves under the scriptural
       bushel, as it were. Here neighbors stay equal,
busy with their seasonal yard tasks,
          avoiding dramatic risks.

But time remains dangerous. A Virginia
       creeper spirals in scarlet up a pine—
now suddenly visible. So years continue,
          forcing our courages to shine,

as together as we face that final event,
       from this middle-class concealment.
A woman sweeping acorns from her drive
          seems daring in staying alive.

Autumn unfurls its banner to the universe:
       the color of time, vector that achieves us
in coming and being, morning and evening,
          spring and fall, loving and leaving.

River-Ruin

A wasp leads my eye above the door.
      The gutter needs repair. Hurricane water
revives a hydrangea, as it now receives
          sun, drying its blooms—lives

as though winters never came here. I hear
      that flooded houses down east are lost,
that mattresses, walls and bedclothes wear
        a stain of human waste.

That place from which I rose toward
      consciousness recedes into nothingness
as I imagine. Spinning time backward,
        I see house and forest in the embrace

of the Neuse, the Tar, the Trent, the Cape Fear:
      each serpent-skin a chrisom
without innocence, stain the land must bear,
        muddy, misplaced baptism.

I sit and watch the light slip west
      as the sun appears to move, each leaf
in process, anticipating frost with loveliest
        mauve-green: small flag of belief

that imperfect ends and beginnings
      testify to the eye as meanings,
explaining themselves as change: turnings
        into oranges, purples, crimsons.

I listen to our brook's new water,
      hearing beauty swirl from disorder.
The waste we make is a past, in weather
        that blue and miasma checker.

I surrender my thoughts to a color,
      mauve-green now tingeing with yellow.
One tree changes, and green October
        burns with a turning I follow.

The Unimaginable

I return a phone call one month late.
   Today our son turns thirty-five.
Shocked at this time we've spent, I appreciate
    the days that leave and arrive.

This morning a shiver touched the yellow-
orange hickory. A poplar's four-
pointed airboats seemed to wallow
    on waves, one sinking before

another would follow. Autumn suspends
   its changes as a leaf descends,
rocking in place in sun and chill,
    the passing imperceptible.

A spider allegorizes its lines
   between trees. Each web shines
a life through the clearing,
    gleaming in sun and ending

in shade. Clouds swirled never
   identically reflect the fever
of sunsets on water. October
    intends to flush before it's over,

celebrating its mock-death with
   trees like florists' sprays, chartreuse as if
adrift beside maroon, orange on azure glaze
    contrast for gazing on *always.*

A Pileated Woodpecker and Toothache

Cedars on the opposite shore raise iron
        filigree against porcelain sky, sun
yellowing poplars. Small birds flicker
           as suddenly a pileated woodpecker,

clapping black-white wing over
        water, swings upside-down
where vines cage his crest, a red fire
           among berries he beaks. Again

he flaps over river, toward a sycamore-
        hollow that echoed his knock before.
Doubled on the glassy rapids,
           he looses his colors in beads.

Delighted and hurt I follow the season
        that combs me in its single direction.
Arrowleaf leans with the current:
           flowing yet staying, bent.

Disturbance from a deep source swirls
        to the surface, boils tighter in circles
that spot time. I watch the turbulent
           Rorschach flux blot

my thoughts almost in focus, like flat
        balloons that wrinkle, then fall apart
and re-form, flicker and bloom
           as if lifting from a flame.

Mind moves over dreams. A woman's hips
        brought tongue to my dry lips
as I left for the dentist—*morning, here,*
           collapsed into a midnight year

when we drove toward the hospital in fear
        in the black car, my brother with infected ear
a lifetime ago. These falling waters veer,
           in a motion our bodies share

along entropy's border. Changing course
        when sun seems lost, I head for the house
and pass a hurricane-broken horizon
            where maples of a new generation

lamp light in yellows and scarlets.
        A feeling like the dissonance in a song
blows through autumn, bronze. I hear its
            colors as I hurry among

these things that change, pained to rejoicing
        by curve of hip, red crest and wing.
I gulp more air and swallow the season raw
            with stinging eye and aching jaw.

Fall Will

Maroon and brown. Blue past a high
      ridge inscribed by a broken oak,
that branches again, refusing to die.
          Horizon of pink and smoke

striped by a waning glow. Wrought iron
      limbs with wiry twigs, closer by,
flying red leaves flecked with brown:
          these dogwoods translucent to sky.

Autumn is moving on now, its slow
      weight felt, spiders sated with moths
while my writing fills with a shadow
          that Earth's shoulder smoothes

across the page. Last light
      where I sit looks slightly pink, faint
illumination for this ink I scrawl
          signing away fall like a will.

National Gallery

From perspective flattened like a map
       the painter has his saint look up.
He has scrawled this journey as a road,
       a winding line to be read.

Mary on her donkey shining blue
       and large diminishes any farther view.
Her infant aureoled among herald angels
       adjusts this cosmos to a stable's

crannies. All's askew with tension—
       this place warped by a higher one.
Colors, primary as for Adam's eye,
       freshen from infinity.

Women's tresses, wheat yellow,
       braid the noon sun without shadow.
Lavender of the two eldest magi
       is snipped from sunset sky.

People and animals from a mountain-middle
       circle toward the centering cradle.
The skewed perspective, down-whirled,
       brings eternity to the world.

Mary's in the foreground, with Joseph
       and Jesu, an ox and a sheep. This hush
in all time is finished with a brush
       of squirrel, a single eyelash.

Natural History

for Marsha and David

The periods in evolution's thermometer
      rise toward Epochs like degrees.
Acrylic layers quicksilver the fever
      of Mesozoic seas.

The goofy music of a cartoon
      accompanies the mosasaur's extinction:
TV at child-level, below bolted teeth
      and eyesocket full of death.

A technician vacuuming in a glass room
      draws me on, his mammals ascendant
on land. Strange herbivores roam,
      nosing toward the elephant.

Skeletons feast on my eyes, wooly
      mammoth rising ten feet above me,
just ten thousand years ago. We were
      beside him, shivered in his fur

at Dolni Vestonice, animal
      also, our houses tusks. Ivory hips
and breasts look endlessly fertile,
      bulging our future like grapes:

those neolithic goddesses. Almost contemporary,
      Neanderthal keeps me from the rest-
room. Overlooking a plaster family,
      a shaman's eyes from his past

dazzle at the mysteries between us.
      His raised hand above these bones marks
near shore of an ocean of process,
      where we're cast by shipwrecks

of ribs and femurs onto an island-present.
      After a meditative piss, I retreat.
The Neanderthal boy, labeled "fully human,"
      foresees his artist's conception.

By the door, a Paleozoic reef lasts as animal
        fern and crenellated fish-lace—
horn of squid and small shell's spiral.
                Paradise. Our lost Atlantis.

Outside, I decide that the meaning's only
        what we carry inside, that the reef
lies drowned in sleep. Sparrows flurry
                over, settle better than belief

in a juniper. The city lies huge with its dead,
        undersea limestone alive in each column,
and humankind, that mad inventor, turreted
                in the Smithsonian, where the season

decorates a conifer with lights.
        I walk among myriads of ascents.
A plane from Washington National wings
                the Monument in its scaffoldings.

Beyond the frontier of a final conquest
        our via dolorosa is an inner West,
where the trek, beyond legible stone,
                leads to ourselves alone.

Prayer at the Solstice

This is the solstice. Overcast.
          Sun, earth, and moon the shortest
distance they can be—sun the closest
               all year, this darkest

hour. Christian is in Puerto Rico
          with his mother, and ill. I fear
for him, my childhood far and near:
               in bed with rheumatic fever,

my father as distant as this sun,
          Mother, close, a full moon
I cannot trust. My bed
               of earth where I suffered

inclines with the northern hemisphere
          away from the golden one, near
if briefly visible. In trouble,
               cold on this path, I call

on a father-sun to recenter
          my universe. Rays enter
my clouded heart; already, light
               leaps warm against

the fright I felt. Christ,
          bring your new year from
an old gloom, renew son-time,
               restore its radiant form.

Christmas by the River

Limbs look warm in waning sun
        high above. Missing my grandson,
hiking away from the grown-up children,
            I find my holiday undone.

Seed balls reflecting on water recall
        the ornaments on a tree miles away,
as the evening swallows only me
            it seems, though air goes gray

over the ridge and over our house also.
        I imagine already the bulb-bright window
I'll see before full dark, then descending
            to rejoin those celebrating

Christ on Earth, whereby I'll place
        myself, out of ill distance and space—
outcast who'll enter his house to feast
            only when sunset's past.

Original evil wills this chill of early
        stars, this barred joy whereby I see
the lights of my family twinkle our tree
            through a wild twig-entropy.

Time Machine

Now winter. Now seed balls from
        the crape myrtle's summer bloom
shine blackberry-brown under ice—
            each copper twig in a case

like vinyl around a wire. The season's
        diagram comes clear. Sparrows on
these glassy limbs flit their old June
            pattern: here, then gone

amid gusts. Below, a juniper wears
        snow-grizzled ice-fur like a bear's.
The palette is muted, tans and grays
            under white or a crystal glaze,

January moving though frozen. Dogwoods'
        stems turn pinker near the buds;
beech leaves hold on, white-tan-alive,
            ready to fall when the curve

of Earth brings jonquils up at their feet,
        like tiny asparagus—good enough to eat
with the eye. So the season deceives
            within barrenness and leaves.

Like a pulse inside an insulating cold,
        a slow sap stirs. But no heat consoled
a white-throated sparrow. It would shiver,
            hop, scratch, and eat, never

looking beyond its dreariest moment.
        So I'm torn between a *now*, when I forget
the past, in this present alone with frost,
            not feeling the Earth go fast—

and the rest, the cosmic radiation I hear
        as through antennas of branches in air.
So memory echoes the illusion
            whereby blossoms come and are gone.

Sometimes, Earth seems a time machine,
      a toy against night in its sunlit spin,
contriving changes with canted poles,
          these seasons for the coloring of our souls.

Before the New Year

Already the year looks new. Pines,
       thin as arrows, vibrate their feathers
as if shot beside these moving waters.
          Each shaft trembles and shines

while our hemisphere points aside, from
       farthest disinclination to be warm—
the river foaming brightly from the west
          as though a cosmic crisis were past.

Angel in the Attic

We strip the tree and return our angel
        to her attic heaven with fiberglass clouds—
this holiday's millennium-cradle
            only ornaments and tinsel shreds.

Then, on New Year's night, we meet
        Christian and his mother at the airport.
He's weak from Puerto Rico and his fever.
            We can't stop hugging each other.

We remember our son, well of his burns,
        home from the hospital. Now our grandson's
with us again, the millennium a fresh space
            for love's unavoidable risk.

Next day, I walk my river path and rejoice.
        Christian is safe with his father.
The Eno rushes in facets of glitter.
            I imagine us riding that surface,

my son and his son canoeing, when Christian's
        older—hoping that, if time runs,
it also pauses and returns.
            I walk and write, the sun's

lower rays a richer color
        where veined by trees. A pileated woodpecker
flaps in light among green-gold pines
            as it imperceptibly dims and shines.

Sun leans across the cobblestone fractal
        rapids, perishably immortal—
stretching its oval on a wet shelf,
            that shines as if aware of itself.

Sun and I send our goodbye look;
        I turn from the creek and go back—
trusting tomorrow's currents to circle
            their unforeseen miracle.

The Vanished Farmhouse

I stopped short, heart tight for my grandson,
      seeing a great horned owl in a pine
against twilight. Two others bowing as in fun
         seemed strange archaic gentlemen.

Cat-eared, they hooted, among needles drained
      of green. The pauper graves,
under a field's found stones, signed
         the poverty that each day leaves.

I found a broken plate in a heap,
      that eighty years wrapped with briars.
Yet, in the weed-scrawled yard, jonquils keep
         pushing up the tips of new years.

Last week, my grandson leaped
      these sunken spaces of woodland burial—
where trees grow, on rows visible in soil.
         The carved words stretched

in the bark of a beech, still legible. Brothers,
      Dan and Paul, had signed their lives
with a knife in nineteen-ten. Others
         will read with later eyes, time curves

always—though the eddy that swirls
      the river with a single life soon vanishes—
love the current that roils and curls
         the shining years. Drowns and replenishes.

Looking Up from the Woodland Clearing

A jet stretches vapor tight,
      trails pink in last high twilight,
though twigs crack the bowl of its flight
        like glaze on this china plate

I've found among first yellow jonquils.
      This family lived and vanished, souls
entangled, I suspect, in these blackberry coils
        like barbed wire. Night falls.

The river rolls and roils, stretched
      through rocks like a village perched
within history. My neighborhood watched
        by a sliver of sunset is matched

by lights coming on, for passengers high
      and beyond me—a future passed into by
far thunder. Tiny and vast, stars swarm,
        humming of times to come.

Family Reunion

I speak the language of others, these clothes
     we wear were worn before and
nakedness is before and after, goes
        to the family's heart. The hand

that catches the two-year-old from falling,
     when the wooden rockinghorse rears,
is everyone's. Laughing and sprawling
        about our rooms, we feel cares

recede, tell tales of desperate parenting
     (that first year's sleeplessness past), nothing
to be pained about, a giving in to the genes
        and time. Then to the scenes

of our separate dreams, that pool our thoughts—
     the anxieties we walk through, snoring, never
ready enough for life or work, the notes
        for our talk in the rival's folder.

Who knows what we'll say, reading
     with the same brain, part of this being,
sharing. I'm one yet many till morning
        and toss unconcerned, sing

whatever song my people's fingers have written,
     since I'm their score. Gestures happen
as we let them, children we've begotten
        bringing us younger children.

Soul Clearing

Through the wind-wrecked leaning
of limbs, I see wild-onion-
green in sun of a clearing.
I wind my way in, overstepping
poison ivy stems, not leafed yet—
each the spine-nerve of a serpent—
to where vine-scrawls spell out *ruin*.
Broken cedars aim in their cones
of briar-sharp greens.
As I stand still to piss,
lost lives course through my penis.
I imagine fathering a family in this place—
then zip up against the blue-green lust, find
deer bones by a cattle-less pasture—
this skull with only one horn.
I know that I'll return,
show these bones to my grandson.

From here I can hear the river,
its going that still remains.
My pulse thumps *life, life*, generation
still on my mind, sun almost down.
I fix pasture-tree coordinates
in mind for future visits.
A snake-sense coils the place I've left
with a horizon like blue scale.
At the dusty road, I cough—
a barn deep brown to my left.
I think that one life is not enough.
Then the windshield holds a sky
pale and gold and chill.
I carry home a skull
in the head, quartz-white, physical,
hard center for this clearing of the soul.

Late March Romance

Three ducks ripple the surface and carve
       their paddling impulse as pieces of curve.
Trailing their vees, they move
          into coves where cherries live.

They double on water, the trees above
       bride-white on each quick wave.
Randy as mating drakes, I swerve
         up winding paths, that preserve

spring bloom. Blossoms resist the ideal.
         Fraying in wind, they won't stand still.
Beheld or not, bloodroot's white, anemones follow,
         then green dots strings of a willow.

This March, the saucer magnolia's
       bloom-lips part, but only for bees. Azaleas
turn pink as a baby's cheeks—viburnum
         like a woman's perfume.

Anthers have exposed their pollen, hour by
       hour, to be rubbed on stigmas by the emissary
bee. In my different season, accidentally
         here, I realize how spring went by,

even when I wasn't around to care.
       My wife and I once happened to share
in beginning three children's lives—then unaware
         how soon the calyx goes bare.

What's left for us now is in our eyes and
       not in our genes. Viburnum's of another mind
but our brief affair only rhymes together
         traits of a flower and weather.

Faces on Waking

Dogwoods blossomed petal leaves,
      marked as with the nails of Christ—
consoling the child in us that grieves
      for every moment lost.

Our grandson growing quickly tall
      hurt our hearts with delight and dread.
I read him rhymes or a fairy tale
      or *The Cat in the Hat* in bed.

I dream their faces, sleepy lover
      of children's lashes that asterisk eyes
to punctuate days, before they alter
      their pure blue of surprise.

The shape of childhood's whisper-wishing
      hurts us with its changing dream
of toy boats, crayfish, stream-exploring—
      the season's uncanny poem.

These petals of dogwoods, really leaves,
      remind us of the palms of Christ.
Time solaces, deceives, and gives
      confusing first and last.

Time hurts us with a tale of days,
      a story over as we discover
how lightning flashes to represent always,
      like the face of a final lover.

The shape of time is a sonata-snake,
      a beginning, middle, and ending thing
that slithers through, as we half awake
      to this Judas music of spring.

The Girl in the Mind

In a garden at the center of the world
       where around her the mountains piled
like reflections in mirrors opposed,
       a little girl played.

Her frock beside the arbor-lattice
       repeated its weave against space—
dark places piercing a surface
       with the delicacy of lace.

Her face along sun-labyrinths
       returns among goldfish and hyacinths—
my cousin in an Easter photograph,
       a negative fading into myth.

She ran through the dream-arch, swing gone
       above her but an arc persisting.
So her music would toll in my bone—
       song without bird to sing.

I'd watched from a brick foundation,
       old ruin flaking like stones from
the world's making. She tripped and I fell on
       this one like myself before time.

She rose unbroken though the flower
       she carried had shattered. Clouds on
the lily pads scattered, without sorrow or
       wind in my mind's monotone.

Storm Grace

The sun pried up a cloud lid ahead,
    and lighted April buds along my road—
their pollen-anthers raveling like thread.

A young woman at a car window, in love,
    held fingers to her chin as her lover drove.
White oaks crowned us with green-silver curve.

Then the Interstate flicked its rough trucks.
    So Stone Cold Steve Austin shakes
his fists, as the crowded area rocks.

This light saw the cables with deeper eyes,
    touched scaffolding and chimneys with praise—
like small things judged from greater size.

The colors of the leaf-crowns wove
    differences into one, like how to live,
in a look of love I hadn't to deserve.

Azaleas by Birdbath

Though the azaleas survive their world,
   Aunt Virginia's garden is sold.
Her daughter has died; yet her favorites
     unfurl their lavender skirts.

The antique silver had gleamed like a star
    for my hungry uncle, who sucked from afar
white bodies and crinolines—cigarette in his mouth,
     dying of this incestuous South.

I transplanted their low-country bushes here.
    They waited a decade, budding near
such bloom, till late-season freezes would come.
     Now color reverses time.

Salmon gowns kick feet to the wind, let
    breezes and bees in, fuchsias illuminate
my sight, sex an act for the eye
     entirely, a fierce stringency,

bodily present, though memory: the day
    I drank a lavender as it lay
on water, and goldfish swam a sham sky,
     that reflected my cousin at play.

Now a goldfinch rivals the earlier marvel,
    fluttering the birdbath. Then a cardinal
condenses from air, these slight lives like
     color for a child—his pure mistake.

So the past survives. The physical's everything
    and nothing, touch a union burning
through years, in tumult of petal and wing
     while afternoon's still morning.

Pine Grove and Railroad

Picking up speed almost
      silently a freight
through the forest
          slices with immense weight

where light holds particulate
      gold in solution. Sun grains
vibrate: time held in panes
        of the windows between pines.

Honeysuckle keeps the sense
      of me first come to this
sun's home. Crow-call is splendid,
        diminishing. Nothing has ended.

Taking Flight

Mountain laurel and rhododendron
  glowed and withered in May's rushing on.
Trout lilies had lighted the slope, in weaker sun
   above March leaves: matchflames gone

in April winds. Anemones bobbed their brighter petals
  on spring-wire stems, among green enamels
of holly and myrtle. White water blurted the syllables
   of downpour, inchoate oracles

of irises to come. Nodding trillium
  and lady slipper called to me in time,
though I missed the river's wild geranium.
   Last evening, a cloud come

with lightning at sunset cast a red glint
  on a pine, so that it burned as at
the end of October, when poison ivy hung it,
   scarlet. Colors ignite

in Earth's quick air, so that I seem already in flight.
  Blooms flicker past in memory, each content
with its moment. Tomorrow, we'll escape
   toward a steadier Europe—

imperial Vienna our hope above a dark
  Atlantic. We'll depart this New World's luck
and landscape, to see by an earlier light—
   completing the season on history's continent.

Ceremony at Heroes' Square

BUDAPEST

The horsemen of Heroes' Square flare
    helmet flaps, over steppes a thousand
years since: a metal legend.
    The angel Michael from his high column
crowns a charioteer's brazen frown
    as Hungarian soldiers from recent wars
place tatty wreaths on tombs of ancestors.
    Those sculpted figures ride wildly above, indifferent,
like the old general with medals, to these dead
    here praised to the skies. This monument
derides the tan-olive uniforms of those led
    as mere boys by its idea. The masquerade's
Magyar gesture toward cloud succeeds.

Strauss in Vienna

This is the Habsburg palace, here
        Francis Joseph fathered his empire.
Here the rococo ceiling convolutes
        the round shriek-notes

into a richness like consciousness.
        Austrian, English, U.S., Polish
we face ourselves in chairs, and polish
        desires on mirrored space.

Red jackets of the Strauss Capel move
        suavely, gold-buttoned breasts heave
as they're paid to do. I think of love
        with the soprano, mind alive

in this reflective room of a dead house.
        This music a moment domes will survive
our bodies. The love-stink of Strauss
        sounds magnificence

in loss, the tone of a race's manyness.
        While she's giving herself to glory, I sense
us gathered within gilt to her groin—
        the time parturient, in ruin.

The Jewish Cemetery and Museum
PRAGUE

Here, denied names are things.
      Cohen, an open hand, rings
true for my next door neighbor.
         I think of his artist daughter.

Rosenkranze, Rosenmannova,
      Rosengarten. All hover,
erased. Schifmann, Waldsteinova.
         I see Hannah Cohen's face—

then can't look without trembling again
      at drawings by children at Terezin.
Lily Bobaschova's "Night" has boat
         and candle for the "dark transport."

Paradise-fish by Ruth Gutmannova
      float out over the time-runes
innocent of how the world means.
         Like balloons among stones.

Prague and Carolina

Our crape myrtle blooms once again.
  This sun's last stand feels Puritan,
westerly, ignorantly American.

The New World's continent atones
  for where Hebrew erupts on stones
of European burials, in letter-skeletons.

Unconsciously, our foliage greens
  in an air washed by last night's rains.
Though a history precedes us into suns,

our might won't allow anymore
  a rapid little Austro-Prussian war,
adjusting the borders of treaty and empire.

We take wars seriously here, defeat
  what we cannot accept. Our settlement,
innocent of faith-strife and serfdom, felt

prior to (and after) the antique terms:
  no Thirty Years War or Diet of Worms
or pogroms, ghettos, or heresy-martyrdoms.

Here light from a cloud leans
  between two hickories, clean as Eden's
first day. The rest of my life begins.

Observing the Sun

I

When balanced on end a needle
      holds all directions, potentially.
Leaning one way it will fall,
         breaking the symmetry.

Committed to a single outcome
      it violates uniform gravity,
like the one-way arrow of time—
         a compass, pointing entropy.

The sun prints my eye as a circle
      with fire-cells shaggily spherical—
Earth's pole inclined from the vertical,
         its orbit imperfect, autumnal.

The spectrum radiating from the sun,
      wherein colors together whiten,
refracts from leaves with the season
         and separates green from the golden.

II

On one of my impulsive down-east trips
      those years ago, chasing an eclipse,
my telescope caught the match of discs,
         and beyond, coronal wisps

against a gray transparence: myth-hair
      a conjunction of our courses let appear.
I dream-saw the cosmos, spinning its rhyme
         in webs from the sun's rim.

The air turned gray like twilight,
      and birds nested trees near the lot
as stars pierced faint and bright
         through a sky illusory as thought.

Then the axis of Earth seemed to lean
        and orbit into seasons by design;
I glimpsed a magenta flame
            around the fountain of time.

Invisible Fence

Will I ever write as freely again
        as lost last year, rhyming when-
ever I breathed? This summer's wren

has raised her brood in the geranium:
        identical pot, a different stem and bloom.
And I'm one year closer to the end of time.

We know God through her/his creation that is
        a love of us, as in our love of these
fellow inhabitants of this time that changes

us as in a pane of light. We do not choose
        to fade as we turn inside it and lose
hopes and images, see possibilities close.

Each day is a border where we walk
        our belief and doubt—a path by a lake
where we note the crushed caterpillar, as clouds take

the needled heads of pines within their rays.
        There the brown man with lighter daughter stays
while I tell him the fierce dog is harmless and he says

that he'll go another way, the Invisible Fence
        not strong enough to trust at once.
I feel his smile touch both of us, and sense

the fraud of the made barrier, difference
        of sex or of how it's practiced, of whence
we've come, the *when* of that elsewhere, the chance

of money, beauty, strength, intelligence,
        poverty or ugliness, while soul intends its glance
through pupils in godly brilliance.

The years really take us *to* ourselves, medium
        we walk in around the lake, in which we come
to love, smelling the houses at suppertime,

the aroma of baking ours. A neighbor who lost his
      wife brought apples home to us—brought the
         mountains
he visited, in their August fragrantness.

I glimpse the whole perspective that I lack
      but seek, and ask that hours, circling back,
remember their beginnings, for pure love's sake.

Against an Ocean Horizon

Missing her father,
she joins me by the gray-blue crashing water.
She likes the kite I fly
and I tow string to my grandson, as shy
at nine as she at nine is direct and full
of lonely talk and beautiful.
The sky's azure, touching ocean
seems the line of summer at autumn.
She sighs like an adult,
telling of the divorce, hurt
but whole in her curled loveliness,
feet quick in the waves that chase us—
friends, since she and her brother
came over when I was grilling, the weather
part stormy, as now. She laughs
as the wind takes away our breaths
and I show her where
my nine-month grandson shines his hair
blowing in sun, and she runs there—
my heart sharply
balancing on pity and beauty.
We all see coming rain
and go in, veils blurring the demarcation
of ocean and sky, transition
itself a blade in my breath,
as I look back the width
of beach to her farewell-waving hand
over the brilliant, cloud-bruised sand.
Later, I watch water on a leaf-tip
clear as her cornea, pregnant to signal
with convex lip
the light's liquid adhesion and fall.

Geese by a Drying Lake

A bluebird and its mate
together on a wire
in late afternoon, as heat
grows less with the light
tolerate stasis a moment
though there's nothing for them but flight.

Wind aloud in the trees stirs
as if crowds of starlings restless
with nesting. Cellulose
strings tie the leaves for a season.
Now in September, water
deserts this scene, a vapor

expanding to a far atmosphere.
By the shrunken lake, where gangly
spring-hatched goslings feed on grass,
three clouds layered like feathers darken
the glass-gray horizon:
the essence of light. And flying.

Come October, will they migrate?
Ganders stretch tall,
remembering: bodily, lyrical,
hatched to feather and parasite.

I watch a wind-sheen turning
on water, then the obsidian pine-shadow.
Above, the sky opens out, a lake of light
to slake my thirst. Eaten by time
I imagine that they already climb,
their young learning horizons also,
lice-winged, immaculate.

Science Fiction Sequence

The toy plane contacts the model
building—surely a special effect,
an advertising trick. The impact
billows in repetition, a fatal

engorging. The windows disappear,
miniature, diminished by distance,
this scale unimaginable: a sequence
signifying hypothetical fear.

We see blindly. Behind the facade
of steel that glows cherry red,
lives evaporate, the numbers of dead
counted on pages within the cloud.

Like the Mount St. Helens explosion
again, it expands. People seem extras
in a director's disaster, insect figures
fleeing as spectacle, non-human—

unless lover or brother or husband.
This event is bad art, motivated
by a robotic, imitated hatred.
Uncannily, the pieces of bodies descend.

This *invisible* means all is abstract,
connotes a remembered war in the sky,
a terrible history, a Twentieth Century—
yet is not Pearl Harbor, attacked.

No pilot looked from his open cockpit,
winging the green pass of farms, *before*.
Once more nothing is learned, war
will determine escalation, permit

bombardiers not to see the detail,
as once beside refinery-circle,
or medieval street become rubble,
of dead girl with hand on her doll.

Engines vortex again, the aliens
we have conceived wedge machined
wings into stratospheres, their blind
windscreens inflict the distanced pains.

TV replays the victory
as of invaders into our sky
against the planet whose breath they fly.
And still we view and cannot see.

Aging/Healing

People take you for granted,
aging, the way you once counted
on your own body. Isn't it a pity?
Actually, you don't feel any.
Examinations expose your skin, the scenes
under their healing machines

just more inscriptions on the brain.
They manage your pain through a vein,
you go under and don't remember.
You feel interest, partisan empathy,
cheering the doctor in his discovery,
spectator, on the side of your own body.

Sure enough, we won. Now I'm better.
But better than what? Not than years ago,
when I'd chainsaw trees, shrub and mow.
Today I oversee my two-man yard crew:
Kenny with his narrow waist
and Popeye forearms, shoveling fast

all afternoon. Tyler tree-trunk sturdy,
heaving the edging machine into the pickup
as easily as I offer the styrofoam cup
of coke. They joke and work
for my respect and check, and mark

this day for me with redefined drive,
mulch edging the gravel, in its arc
beyond the pergola, as a perfected curve.
Now the landscape-lights shine newly on
red-fresh pinestraw when the sun has gone.
My wife sees my pleasure in being alive.

As I talk she says that I look young.
I'm pleased to be in the world, among
others heartier, taking part in the song
that all beings sing together—not the one
wielding shovel or saw anymore, but upon
the same ground. I'm sleepier earlier,

but so what? I nap and forget, reader
of the body's story, playing follow the leader.
The light at this end of time seems mellower.
Sun seems to touch the renewed yard
with affection, an enhanced regard.

The old have their place in the world,
even if finally it's a hole. The memory
of pain fades, the fright passes, the agony
ends, eventually. This is to say
that the things I dread can't spoil
this brilliant decline of afternoon, the toil

of words, of imagined and real, the forms
that lines assume, the rhymes as they throng
my paper, though mirrors say "no longer young."
That old dream. Image of self, the perfection
of a look or an act, lonely exaltation,
once, of power in the body. These different times.

I live among others, for others, see myself
in sidelong glances as the fallible granddad
who forgets his glasses. But they sit for me to read:
the grandsons, the students, fellow professors of breath
for whom delight is what we discover, together.
I don't see why it can't go on forever.

Game Store Near the Airport

My heart in enlightenment towered
as the sun lowered, while traffic poured
in impatience and eagerness West toward
no end in view except evening stasis—aspired
as if to grasp an unrepresented dream. Desired
by the brain as bodily image, the hard-wired
beauty now hovered before: evolved reward
and ideal, to be possessed and also adored.
I'd found the labyrinth-looks and formula stored
in electronic memory, a magic with fire and sword
offered in games for my grandson. Dragons reared
out of dungeons and a king returned, empowered
by legend, restored with sword, to be lord
of the embowered maiden. Fortresses towered
above plains of battle and a river poured
its years between statued giants, toward
the sun on ocean. The quester's path aspired
from spaces on Earth, into a light for itself desired.
An airliner soared the sunset, the passengers wired
into music or movies, while outside the lord
sun showered his rays, that the liner adored
with silver skin. An entelechy stored
in story and symbol fused flame and sword;
the invention of metal and flying reared
the gathered hearts against the light, empowered—
a farther clearness their keen reward.
The game-language spoke to my grandson, who gazed
at the sword-like liner as the sunset blazed.
I consoled his wish with stories wrought
out of history, telling perhaps of the shaped flame
hammered through the long dark as the shape sought,
a way of beholding, of illuminating beauty and name.

Not Knowing

Not knowing we lived lightly,
in liners ascending with the day
aluminum gleaming into sun legibly

Not knowing we trusted
our hearts to towers, aspiringly met
among papers in deals with vapors brilliant at sunset

Not knowing we rose
winging dawn into distance, arcing
gravity on metals immune against falling

Not knowing we counted
the pieces in dust, entreaties unsaid,
unsigned, the deeds undone, discontenanced lovers unlaid

Not knowing we wept
in smoke, washed our eyes and unfurled
an anger striped red above the world

Not knowing we cast
tears into the void, a horizon of good-byes, eyes
disappearing with windows, twin absences in series

Not knowing we armed
against sorrow flinging new wings conceived
with dark eggs into air between mountains, grieved

Not knowing we haunted
the hurt in others, investigating
our vulnerable treasures, unvalued, the banners trembling

Not knowing we kept this best
for humankind carelessly, the meaning we were not flying
before us, then—now in our eyes, only stars ideas and
    burning

www.ingramcontent.com/pod-product-compliance
Lightning Source LLC
Chambersburg PA
CBHW021348090426
42742CB00008B/786

* 9 7 8 0 8 0 7 1 3 1 2 7 5 *